CELEBRATING HOLIDAYS

Juneteenth

by Rachel Grack

BELLWETHER MEDIA · MINNEAPOLIS, MN

Note to Librarians, Teachers, and Parents:

Blastoff! Readers are carefully developed by literacy experts and combine standards-based content with developmentally appropriate text.

Level 1 provides the most support through repetition of high-frequency words, light text, predictable sentence patterns, and strong visual support.

Level 2 offers early readers a bit more challenge through varied simple sentences, increased text load, and less repetition of high-frequency words.

Level 3 advances early-fluent readers toward fluency through increased text and concept load, less reliance on visuals, longer sentences, and more literary language.

Level 4 builds reading stamina by providing more text per page, increased use of punctuation, greater variation in sentence patterns, and increasingly challenging vocabulary.

Level 5 encourages children to move from "learning to read" to "reading to learn" by providing even more text, varied writing styles, and less familiar topics.

Whichever book is right for your reader, Blastoff! Readers are the perfect books to build confidence and encourage a love of reading that will last a lifetime!

This edition first published in 2019 by Bellwether Media, Inc.

No part of this publication may be reproduced in whole or in part without written permission of the publisher. For information regarding permission, write to Bellwether Media, Inc., Attention: Permissions Department, 6012 Blue Circle Drive, Minnetonka, MN 55343.

Library of Congress Cataloging-in-Publication Data

Names: Koestler-Grack, Rachel A., 1973- author.
Title: Juneteenth / by Rachel Grack.
Description: Minneapolis, MN : Bellwether Media, Inc., 2019. | Series: Blastoff! readers: Celebrating Holidays | Includes bibliographical references and index. | Audience: K-3.
Identifiers: LCCN 2017056565 (print) | LCCN 2017058287 (ebook) | ISBN 9781626177888 (hardcover : alk. paper) | ISBN 9781681035178 (ebook)
Subjects: LCSH: Juneteenth–Juvenile literature. | Slaves–Emancipation–Texas–Juvenile literature. | African Americans–Texas–Galveston–History–Juvenile literature. | African Americans–Anniversaries, etc.–Juvenile literature. | African Americans–Social life and customs–Juvenile literature. | Slaves–Emancipation–United States–Juvenile literature.
Classification: LCC E185.93.T4 (ebook) | LCC E185.93.T4 K64 2019 (print) | DDC 394.263-dc23
LC record available at https://lccn.loc.gov/2017056565

Editor: Paige Polinsky   Designer: Andrea Schneider

Printed in the United States of America, North Mankato, MN.

Table of Contents

Juneteenth Is Here!

People gather around a stage. They watch a **historical reenactment**.

historical reenactment

4

An army general says, "All **slaves** are free." Everyone cheers! It is Juneteenth!

What Is Juneteenth?

Juneteenth marks the end of slavery in the United States. It is also called Freedom Day.

Many people honor
African-American **culture**.

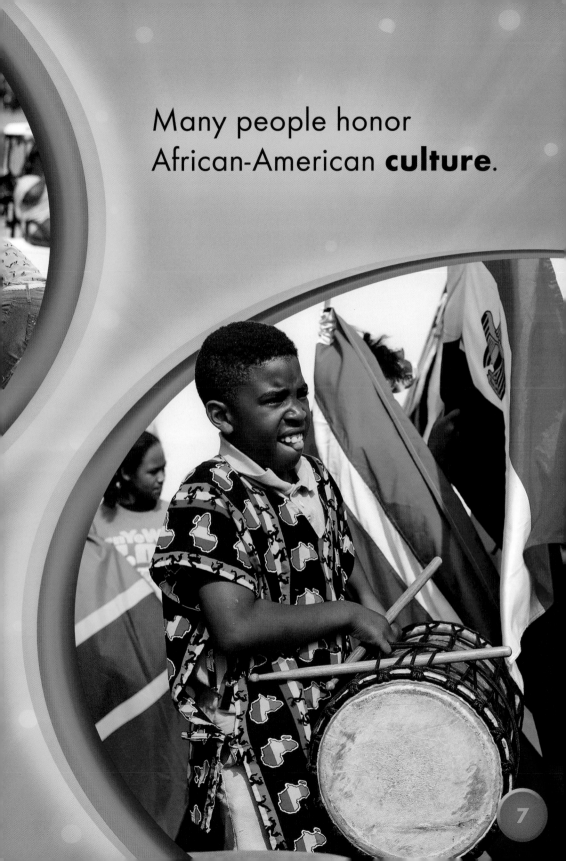

Who Celebrates Juneteenth?

African Americans **observe** this holiday. Other people can join in, too.

It is an **official** holiday
in most states.

The United States used to practice slavery.

In 1863, President Abraham Lincoln's **Emancipation Proclamation** freed the last slaves. But the news spread slowly.

Abraham Lincoln

The news reached Galveston, Texas, last. The state's 250,000 African-American slaves became free on June 19, 1865.

They chose to celebrate
this day every year!

Time to Celebrate

Juneteenth takes place on June 19. Its name comes from this date.

Texas made it a holiday in 1980. Other states followed.

Juneteenth Timeline

1863	Emancipation Proclamation frees the last slaves
June **1865**	News of the Emancipation Proclamation reaches Galveston, Texas
December **1865**	13th Amendment ends slavery in the United States
1980	Texas makes Juneteenth a state holiday

Juneteenth Traditions!

African Americans celebrate their **heritage** on this day.

Many go to church. They
sing **spirituals**. They
remember their **ancestors**.

Some cities hold parades. People fly a special flag. They listen to **speeches** about the past. They also share hope for the future.

Make a Juneteenth Flag

Many people raise the Juneteenth flag on this holiday. The star stands for hope rising on a new day.

What You Need:
- red and blue construction paper
- scissors
- glue stick
- white chalk
- hair spray

What You Do:

1. Cut the red construction paper in half the long way.

2. Glue one strip of the red paper onto the bottom half of the blue paper.

3. Use the chalk to draw a 12-pointed star on the paper as shown.

4. Draw a 5-pointed star inside the first star. Color it in.

5. Lightly spray the flag with hair spray. This will keep the chalk from rubbing off.

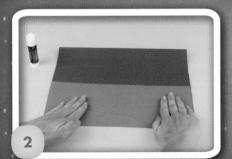

2

4

19

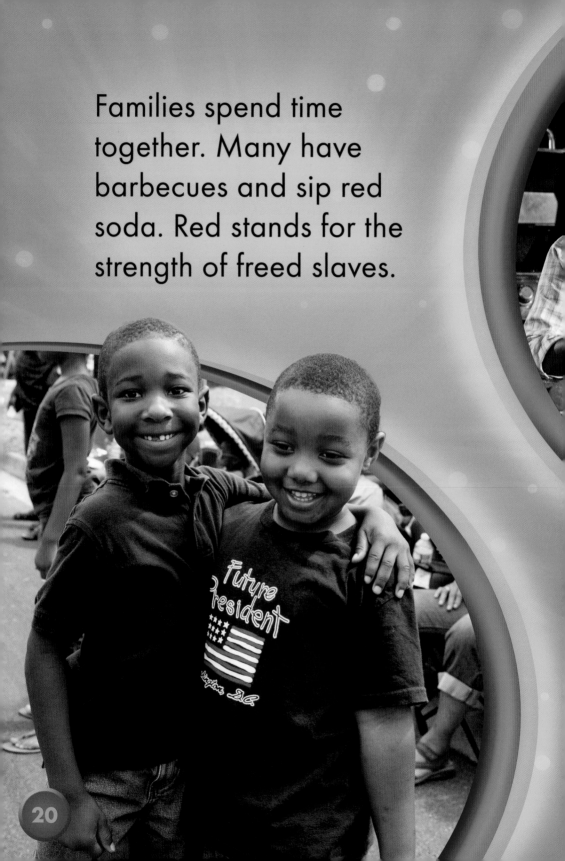

Families spend time together. Many have barbecues and sip red soda. Red stands for the strength of freed slaves.

People honor this strength.
They celebrate freedom!

Glossary

ancestors—relatives who lived long ago

culture—the traditions and way of life of a group of people

Emancipation Proclamation—a law by the president to free slaves of certain states

heritage—the history of a person or group of people

historical reenactment—a play that acts out events from history

observe—to celebrate

official—publicly known

slaves—people who are considered property

speeches—talks given to a group of people; on Juneteenth, people might give speeches about African-American heritage.

spirituals—religious songs sung by African slaves

To Learn More

AT THE LIBRARY
Cooper, Floyd. *Juneteenth for Mazie*. North Mankato, Minn.: Picture Window Books, 2015.

Ponto, Joanna, and Angela Leeper. *Juneteenth*. New York, N.Y.: Enslow Publishing, 2017.

Smith, Maximilian. *The History of Juneteenth*. New York, N.Y.: Gareth Stevens Publishing, 2016.

ON THE WEB
Learning more about Juneteenth is as easy as 1, 2, 3.

1. Go to www.factsurfer.com.

2. Enter "Juneteenth" into the search box.

3. Click the "Surf" button and you will see a list of related web sites.

With factsurfer.com, finding more information is just a click away.

Index